MORE PRAISE FOR THE ASCE

I love practical but deep tools. I found one in *The Ascended Life* by Brian Orme! He has laid out a simple 21-day guide to get readers to live a deeper and more connected life with God, and it is full of practical connection points like declarations and prayers. I think this is exactly the kind of tools we need in this social media-driven, high-paced age during which we have to be this deliberate in setting apart real time for a real God journey. This book will frame it for you.

Shawn Bolz
Author of *Translating God*
www.bolzministries.com

In his new 21-day guidebook, *The Ascended Life*, Brian Orme has created a wonderfully crafted experience for those wanting a daily dose of revelation and empowerment. If you want to know more about your identity, the full power of the cross and your co-union with Christ, this guidebook is for you. Each revelation and declaration will enhance your relationship with the Lord and others, and propel you to greater heights in His love!

Georgian Banov
Founder of Global Celebration

Brian Orme's book *The Ascended Life* is a 21-day spiritual, emotional and mental detox. Brian's unique way of expressing revelation washes out the sludge of false identity and the dirt of religious self-help, thrusting the reader into the wide open spaces of the unreasonable grace of God.

This book is designed for the adventurer: Every sentence provides a new invitation to explore the goodness and generosity of the Father, Son and Holy Spirit. Each day's declaration elevates the declarer to new heights of hope and joy. I promise you, after 21 days of The Ascended Life, you will see "It is finished" in a whole new light.

David Crone
Senior Leader of The Mission Vacaville
Author of *Prisoner of Hope*, *Decisions that Define Us*,
Declarations That Empower Us, and *The Power of Your Life Message*

There are many ways to approach living. Brian provides insights on how life in Jesus causes us to live something very different. There is more available to us than we've yet experienced. *The Ascended Life* gives you needed understanding to live from your highest point to unlock your highest potential. You will enjoy what you gain from going through this study over and over again.

Eric Reeder
Founder/President of RISEmovement
Founder/Professor of RISEinstitute
www.generationsrise.com

I can't tell you enough how much I enjoyed reading Brian Orme's book, *The Ascended Life*. I liked it for several reasons. The first is that I have known the Orme's for nearly two decades now and I can tell you clearly that the message of this book is a reality in how they have lived out Kingdom life values. It is a reflection of not just what they believe, but how they do everyday life. Brian and Cecilee are some of our greatest heroes in the faith, because they live their lives with purpose and determination to experience the fullness of the Kingdom, while taking as many people along on the journey as possible.

Second, I am excited about this book because it gives the readers a fresh view of how to recalibrate their lives to come out of faulty mindsets, and to understand just how vested the Lord Jesus Christ is in His commitment towards moving us into a lifestyle of freedom and faith.

It is a wonderful 21-day guidebook written to challenge you to shake off faulty beliefs and ideologies about how you may have viewed God in a wrong way. Ultimately, it is a call for us to be rooted in the goodness of God and to understand fully that He is for us! It is a great read for anyone who wants to experience the fullness of God and to truly reach a reality of *The Ascended Life*!

Shannon Schreyer
Senior Leader of God's Place
www.godsplace.us

Perspective changes everything! In his new book, *The Ascended Life*, Brian Orme challenges us to shake off the mediocrity of the basic principles of this world as we journey into living from a higher vantage point. More than a book of theories, this straight-forward 21-day guidebook is filled with practical truths from the path that the author has been walking for years. Brian shows us that being seated together with Christ is more than positional theology, it's a way of life. So prepare for a mind-shift as you travel towards the transformation that comes from a renewed mind.

Brad McKoy
Author of Culture of the Few
www.cultureofthefew.com

I have known Brian for many years now and I have the privilege of calling him one of my best friends. I've had the honor of ministering alongside him and also have been able to walk with him through many different life situations. Through it all, I have had a front row seat to watch someone walk out the ascended lifestyle in everyday life.

When an author writes a book from mere information, it has the ability to teach and inspire us. However, when an author writes from a place of revelation, it has the ability to transform us. Brian has written a 21-day, revelatory heart-map that will guide you to live out the ascended lifestyle. I wholeheartedly endorse this book, and believe it is one of the most impactful books I have ever read on the resurrection life of a follower of Christ. Get ready to step into the life you were created for!

Matt Gonzales
Co-Senior Leader of Innovation Church, Co-Founder of Innovation School of Transformation, Founder of Kingdom Culture Ministries
www.icstockton.org

For almost a decade, I have had the privilege of observing Brian's life under a magnifying glass-first as a friend, then mentor, and for the past several years as a spiritual father. In all of our richly authentic conversations and shared, everyday covenant living, it has been strengthening to see a man who is unrelenting in his resolve to truly follow Christ, without a roadmap other than moment by moment direction from God. The anointing on his book comes from the deep well of the sufferings of Christ he has drunk from and the joy that follows. Brian gives a clear, powerful approach to developing an intimacy as a Son or Daughter of God that requires living outside the box, risk-taking that cleanses the soul, and Truth-seeking that supersedes logic and analysis. I highly encourage you to take the time to read these words, which are life-changing in their simplicity and profound revelation.

Eric Waterbury
Founder of World Changers

THE ASCENDED LIFE

A 21-Day Guidebook to Co-Ascended Thinking & Breakthrough

Brian Orme

Foreword by Dan McCollam, author of *God Vibrations*

iBorme.com

THE ASCENDED LIFE

A 21-Day Guidebook to Co-Ascended Thinking & Breakthrough

The Ascended Life is a 21-day guidebook that will help bring awareness of your co-ascension with Christ, elevate your thinking, and empower you to live from a higher vantage point.

© Copyright 2016 Brian Orme

www.iborme.com

ISBN- 978-09977856-0-9

Editor: Elizabeth Chung
Cover Design and Formatting: Whitney Zhu and Raechel Wong

Acknowledgements

I would like to start by saying thank you to my wife, Cecilee, the most important person in my life. You are one of the strongest people I know and have taught me so much about endurance, kindness, and classiness. You are an amazing representation of Jesus. There is no one better than you to laugh, cry, or take a leap of faith with. I love you.

Thank you to my children, Eowyn and Liam, who never cease to amaze me. Your creativity, genuine love for others, discernment, humor, and confidence have changed my world and will do the same to everyone you meet. I love you.

I would like to honor my parents, Ralph and Mary Jean Orme. I am very grateful to have had loving parents that modeled compassion, love for God, and a strong work ethic. Dad, I will see you soon.

I would like to acknowledge the following people (in no particular order) who have encouraged, challenged, and inspired me in the journey of life: Shannon and Nancy Schreyer, my in-laws Bob and April Basura, Eric Waterbury, Matt Gonzales, Sean Cherry, Banning Liebscher, Erica Greve, and my grandma, Virginia Boynton, who is with the cloud of witnesses.

I would like to say thank you to all the spiritual sons and daughters God has brought into my life. You have all taught me so much about the Father's love, the fullness of the Kingdom, and so much more. I am humbled and honored to be in your lives and watch you change the world.

I would like to say thank you to the following heroes in the Body of Christ; you have been an amazing example and influence in my life: Bill Johnson, Harold Eberle, Jonathan Welton, Dan McCollam, Georgian and Winnie Banov, David and Deb Crone, Sean Smith, and Bobby Conner.

CONTENTS

Preface i
Day 1: Love High 1
Day 2: Divinely Natural 4
Day 3: Now It's Up to You…Not 7
Day 4: Bold is Gold 10
Day 5: Sailing the Worth-Ship 13
Day 6: False Covering 17
Day 7: Restful Revelation 20
Day 8: Prophetic Tension 23
Day 9: A Whole Lot of Ology 26
Day 10: Gold Dust or Bust 29
Day 11: Seeing from Honoring 32
Day 12: Acts 2 as New 35
Day 13: Patient Ascension 38
Day 14: A + S = Drop Dead 41
Day 15: Pain and Pursuit 43
Day 16: Circular Travel 46
Day 17: Lain 49
Day 18: Living in the Logos 52
Day 19: Diving Deep 55
Day 20: Don't Settle 58
Day 21: Bending the Sending 61
Concluding Thoughts 64
About the Author: 66

PREFACE

Starting at a young age, I would climb anything. Maybe it's a boy thing, but I wanted to traverse upwards as much as possible. There was just something exhilarating about finding the best possible vantage point in a high place.

While growing up in Michigan, I found a treasure trove of trees awaiting my ascension into their branches of splendor. Climbing them was one of my favorite things to do. One time I found myself at the top of a tall one, probably 60 feet above the ground. I perched victoriously over the branches, gazing down upon the lush forest and nearby pond. That confidence quickly faded when I heard the cracking sound of a branch about to give up on life. I began to descend swiftly, making sure to hit every branch on the way down. It is quite miraculous that I didn't break any bones, sustain major injuries, or even die.

I was willing to risk in order to have a better vantage point.

When you have a high viewpoint, you can take it all in. My wife Cecilee and I lived in Salt Lake City, Utah, for eight years and absolutely loved the mountains. One of our favorite hikes was breathtakingly beautiful in the fall. Once, we were heading up this trail and I was intensely focused on ascending the mountain. I was blazing up the switchbacks and then realized I had left Cecilee in my selfish dust. I heard her yell, "Brian, I am down here and you're missing the view."

When I stopped to look, I was overwhelmed by beauty. The vibrant colors of the changing trees, the endless vistas, and of course, my beautiful wife. I had been so focused on the destination that I'd nearly missed the transformation of creation all around me. I walked back down to rejoin Cecilee and we continued to meander up the trail. We made it to the top and stared in silence at the utterly mind-blowing grandeur.

In Christ, we have the highest vantage point possible. It is called being seated with Christ in the heavenly realms (Ephesians 2:6). We are in Him and He is in us, meandering the trails of life together. In Christ we were co-crucified, co-buried, and co-resurrected—and we *co-ascended*.

The Ascended Life is a 21-day guidebook to help you see from a higher perspective. Height brings sight. It's a journey to accomplish a mental relocation to throne-life realities with daily bits of breakthrough that will challenge, inspire, and encourage.

Let's begin to live and function from our co-ascension in Christ. It's a place above the cares and affairs of a world that we are not of. A place from which we can create the greatest impact on Earth. We were made new for this ascended life, and walking in it will transform how we live today and tomorrow.

FOREWORD

Researchers from a 2009 study at University College London found that the minimum time to establish a new habit-or break an old one-was 21 days.

For 25 years I lived as a pastor, worship leader, and itinerant speaker who only knew the cross on the basis of forgiveness. "Christ died for me" is a glorious reality that brings the first light of the kingdom of God into view in the form of forgiveness from sin. The problem with living from the position of merely being forgiven, however, is that you can only relate to God on the basis of your failure and His mercy. Forgiveness alone does not create a great forum for true communion because it keeps me a helpless beggar.

The greater reality of the cross is in the fact that "Christ died as me." I died with Him to be freed from the very nature of sin and now by God's grace am filled with the very fullness of God. Thus, the cross is a work of forgiveness and freedom that takes me to a place of immeasurable fullness. Many, like my own experience, have identified with the work of forgiveness but not fullness. They have come through Christ, the Way, and are now merely standing "in the way," never having truly entered into the fuller blessings of the glorious kingdom life.

Biblically, I am now convinced that our identification with Christ does not stop at the cross. We enter the ground with Him in the identification of baptism for a closure to our former existence. In the identification with His resurrection we are raised up and made alive together with Him. Too many Christians live with a present-tense relationship with sin and a future tense relationship with resurrection. As I mentioned earlier, this was my position as a church leader for 25 years. The Scripture puts our relationship with sin in the past tense and our relationship with resurrection in the present tense. Though a greater physical resurrection benefit awaits us in an even more glorious future, we are now made alive together in His resurrection. It's time to reset our spiritual clocks and get on the resurrection side of the cross.

We must learn to pull as hard on the blessings side of the cross as we have on the forgiveness side. On the forgiveness side of the cross we get our debts paid; on the resurrection side of the cross we get our checks signed. Forgiveness zeroes out our negative balance, but freedom and fullness make deposits into our account. The new nature together with God's forgiveness gives us a greater place of fellowship with God as true sons and daughters.

Yet, our identification does not stop at the resurrection. When we entered into divine union with Christ at the cross it also made us one in His ascension. This is how we find ourselves now seated in heavenly places in Christ Jesus (Ephesians 2:6). Some may ask, "What will be my proximity to His throne in heaven?" What a silly question. I am now seated in Christ, not near Him, but in Him. From this position everything looks radically different.

Ascension reveals a very different me. I find the secrets of my own new creation in this identification with the ascended Christ. I discover an eternal heavenly identity that redefines my shabby, earthly, internal one. I also see the world and my circumstances from a vastly different view seated in heavenly places.

Paul's writings encourage us, *"Since, then, you have been raised with Christ, set your hearts on things above, where Christ is, seated at the right hand of God. Set your mind on things above, not on earthly things."* (Colossians 3:1-2)

This is the beauty of Brian's book, *The Ascended Life*. It begins the journey of refocusing your heart and mind on living from heaven's perspective. Too many Christians live from Earth waiting to go to heaven. Jesus came from heaven, lived on Earth, and prepared for His return. This is the pattern of a believer pursuing the ascended life: we must live from heaven, on Earth, toward heaven.

I have known Brian for several years now. He is a brilliant thinker and carries an unusual level of courage for embracing deeper revelation. I have met the lives that Brian and Cecilee have impacted in their campus ministry on one of the most intellectually elite campuses in America. Their disciples are transformed believers with a deep passion for the living Christ and true revelation.

I'm convinced that the author and this book carry a weighty gift for a radical renewing of the mind. If studies say that a person can begin to change a habit or a mind set in no less than 21 days, then this journal will be an essential roadmap for crossing over from the wrong side of the cross to the more glorious path of the ascended life.

I find the devotions in this book extremely inspiring and the declarations and meditations hugely helpful. This is the book I wish I had read early in my own journey of faith. Thank you, Brian, that others can begin to find in 21 days what it took me 25 years to discover. May your journey of identification with the ascended Jesus take you from glory to glory with ever-increasing glory.

Dan McCollam
The Mission, Vacaville, California
International Director of Sounds of the Nations
Author of *Basic Training in Prophetic Activation*, *A Prophetic Company*, *A Song For Seven Mountains*, *My Super Powers* (Series for kids on spiritual gifts), *God Vibrations* and more.

Day 1: Love High

Love is essential to all life. Love is a person. Love is the foundation of all creation. We were made not just for love; we were made from love. God took a piece of His heart and created us. Our mother's womb is not our origin; we just passed through it. Our origin is Christ. We came from love.

Thus, it pains His heart when His kids don't live from His love. Without love, the body doesn't exist. He wants to exist through us, love through us, and utterly flood us with a greater capacity to love.

The Father's love reveals the horrific loneliness of individualism. The concept of "I" died at the cross, and we came out on the other side as "we." In Christ, we don't know when we end and He begins. We are one. That's why Paul said in Galatians 2:20, *"It's no longer I that lives, but Christ in me."*

WE WERE MADE NOT JUST FOR LOVE; WE WERE MADE FROM LOVE.

Our oneness with Christ shines when we choose to love. Love is not optional when you want to live in truth. There's no love outside of light, and no light outside of love (1 John 2). Love and light flow from the life of God. They are all entwined together.

Because we came from Jesus, we arrived on this earth without fear. Since fear is learned "here," our journey on this earth is to learn to love and, as a result, unlearn fears. People say that knowledge is power, but fearlessness is true power.

Our physical world has three spatial dimensions. But the love of Jesus is described as having four dimensions: length, width, depth, and height (Ephesians 3:18). Love causes increased awareness of our co-ascension into heavenly dimensions. Heaven and earth meet at love.

Love deep and you'll soar high.

Speak Up: Declaration

I declare I was made from love and for love. I have no idea where I end and He begins. Oneness has been established through the cross. It's no longer I that lives, but Christ in me. I reject the loneliness of individualism and isolationism and embrace the unceasing love poured over me by the Father, Jesus, and Holy Spirit. I walk in love and thus, I walk in the light. I receive His perfect love today that drives out every fear, every worry, all anxiety, and the perceived need to overthink. I give away all His love that is flowing toward and through me.

THINK DEEP: MEDITATION

1 Corinthians 13, 1 John 2, 1 John 4:8, Ephesians 3:18

DAY 2: DIVINELY NATURAL

The domain of darkness is cheap and runs on a very tight budget centered around lack. One of its favorite tools is intimidation, where it dispatches a lying, deceiving spirit to fool people into giving up. This way, darkness can gain territory without incurring expenses.

To their chagrin, 2 Peter 1:4 states that we have become partakers in "the divine nature." Of course, this refers to Jesus' nature in which we've been fully immersed. Because our nature is Jesus' nature, darkness is infuriated that we reflect the One they couldn't keep down.

Beauty corresponds to truth. Our physical bodies are a constant reminder to Satan of the image of God. For that very reason, the enemy has chosen the human body as one of his major arenas of battle because it's God's crowning creative genius. You're the best idea God ever had.

Our eyes and ears remind the enemy that we can see and hear God. This is why Satan seeks to cause blindness and deafness both physically and spiritually. We have been given a new spiritual nature, not a new logical nature. It is now natural to hope, and unnatural to be skeptical. Belief is natural. Unbelief is foreign.

> **EVERY TIME WE CREATE, IT'S AN ATTACK ON THE DOMAIN OF DARKNESS, WHICH HAS NO CREATIVE ABILITY.**

Unlike God, Satan cannot create. He can only distort and twist that which has been created. One of the highest expressions of our new nature in Christ is creativity. Every time we create, it's an attack on the domain of darkness, which has no creative ability. To say we are not creative is absurd.

We are one with Christ. As we dwell in His nature, His fullness makes us complete and brings us into a place of authority and rule over the enemy.

New nature. New life. Divinely natural living.

SPEAK UP: DECLARATION

I declare that I am the best idea God ever had. My nature is His nature. I choose hope and reject skepticism. I am a believer, and I reject unbelief. I can hear God and I can see God. I declare health over my body, for it is the temple of the Holy Spirit. My body exists because love exists.

I cannot help but be creative, for the Creator's nature has been shared with me. God's fullness has completed me and His authority has commissioned me. I destroy the works of the devil.

THINK DEEP: MEDITATION

Exodus 35:30-33, John 10:27, 2 Peter 1:1-4, Ephesians 2:10

DAY 3:
NOW IT'S UP TO YOU...NOT

There is a common phrase that's uttered when people are given the opportunity to accept Jesus: "Come as you are, no matter what you've done. God will forgive you." This is true; we can come as we are. No matter what we have done, it won't prevent us from receiving the furious love of the Father.

Very quickly after the "come as you are" comment, however, there comes a nonverbal message. It basically implies, "Now it's up to you to stay forgiven." Now that you have freely entered into the Kingdom, your works are going to need to go into hyperdrive to keep yourself clean.

That's rubbish. Forgiveness is a gift. You've got to understand that when you came to Jesus and asked Him to come in, you were already forgiven. You received the gift of forgiveness and all it's benefits when you chose to believe. Every person in darkness is forgiven, they just haven't chose to believe yet. If we believe otherwise, then we have to come to the conclusion that God forgives in installments.

Jesus' sacrifice was once and for all time. His forgiveness was once and for all time. After all, the word "forgive" means to "send away." Your sin hasn't merely been overlooked, it has been permanently abolished and removed. It is not up to you to stay forgiven. It is up to you to focus on the truth of His forgiveness, purity, righteousness, and much more that you were given through the finished work of Jesus.

In light of this, confession isn't the means to attain forgiveness. It isn't transactional; it's relational. Confession reflects the agreement of your forgiveness, the vulnerability to acknowledge that you need help, and the receiving of His grace to reign in every area of life.

YOUR SIN HASN'T MERELY BEEN OVERLOOKED, IT HAS BEEN PERMANENTLY ABOLISHED AND REMOVED.

Grace enables what it commands. You have power to live victoriously over sin. It is easy to live out of righteousness when you realize you're a slave to it.

We are supposed to fix our eyes on Jesus. Gazing in

any other direction will cause us to feel things that are outside the mind of Christ (shame, guilt, condemnation, and so forth). We must rest in the reality of a freely given gift: forgiveness.

Now, we have the incredible opportunity to freely give what we have freely received. There will be plenty of opportunities in life to offer forgiveness to others.

How beautiful would it be to get to a place in life where we can't wait to forgive again?

SPEAK UP: DECLARATION

I declare I was forgiven once and for all time. Forgiveness was and is a gift. I didn't earn it, I freely received it. Thank you, Jesus, for Your finished work that has changed my life. I declare that shame, guilt, and condemnation are not found in You nor me. I am free in Christ. I forgive anyone (insert names) who has hurt me. They don't owe me anything. I freely give away what I have freely been given. I speak life over all who have wronged me. I love to forgive. It reminds me of all I have been forgiven of.

THINK DEEP: MEDITATION

Colossians 2:13, Hebrews 7:27, Hebrews 10:18

DAY 4: BOLD IS GOLD

What is boldness? Where does it come from? Confidence is another word used to describe boldness. Confidence is simply the result of abiding in Jesus. We can't help but be confident when we focus on our oneness with Jesus.

When Peter and John stand before the council in Acts 4 and release some heavy revelation, the council is astounded by the fact that these men are "uneducated," and they recognize they had been "with Jesus." Despite the fact that they seemed unqualified, Peter and John's confidence to speak up and make an impact came from abiding in Jesus.

Many say that knowledge is power. That is a lie. Fearlessness is power. Who cares what you know if you don't do anything alongside it that requires boldness? At that point, the knowledge is irrelevant. God didn't give us fear, so we should not accept it into our lives and allow it to prevent us from walking out in boldness.

Our intellect will not lead us into places requiring boldness. It will lead us into controllable, manageable, and predictable spaces. The Holy Spirit, on the other hand, will lead us into impossible situations that

MANY SAY THAT KNOWLEDGE IS POWER. FEARLESSNESS IS POWER.

demand boldness. He will take us where we are in over our heads, above our pay grades, and beyond what we are qualified to do (according to the world's standards). This is where we are humbled in our weakness and captivated by His strength.

Love, hope, and faith follow a powerful flow. Everything starts with the truth that we are loved. When we know He loves us, we can confidently hope that He will come through for us. According to 2 Corinthians 3:12, *"Since we have such a hope, we are very bold."* Boldness flows from hope. It's not about desperation, but about expectation. If we abound in hope, we will abound in boldness. If hope is deferred, then our boldness will be too.

Our hope, or expectancy, opens the door to certainty (faith). Faith without hope is dead. It is the nature of God to believe and expect. Since we have been given His nature, it is natural for us to believe and expect.

When we know we are loved, we can hope (expect), which then allows us to apply faith (certainty) to see the Kingdom of God demonstrated.

As His beloved children, we have been made with the righteousness of God in Christ. Proverbs 28:1 says, *"The righteous are as bold as a lion."* The foundation of boldness is righteousness. It isn't founded in personal bravery or personality. It is founded in identity. He made us right so we can do what is right.

We have been made righteous, and therefore we have been made bold. We don't have to conjure up boldness. Our gaze is to be set on what He has done. Remember what He has given and forget what He has forgiven. One of the meanings of boldness is "leaving a witness that something deserves to be remembered" (http://biblehub.com/greek/3954.htm). If we are going to leave a mark on this world, it will require us to leave safety and predictability behind.

It is time to roar. It is time to leave a legacy that will be remembered.

SPEAK UP: DECLARATION

The Father's love flows toward me at all times. Hope is alive and well. Faith is available at all times. In Christ, I am confident in every area of life. He knows who I am, so I know whose I am. I reject fear, for it is not my portion. I embrace impossible situations knowing I have been given the same Spirit that raised Jesus from the dead. I declare that in Christ I am righteous. Therefore, I am as bold as a lion.

THINK DEEP: MEDITATION

Proverbs 28:1, 2 Corinthians 3:12

DAY 5:
SAILING THE WORTH-SHIP

Worship with music is a powerful thing. Music opens doors to invisible realities, which are good or bad. Worship opens up windows to God's promises set aside for us. When we make the choice to worship in the midst of our circumstances, our perception changes and our gaze is drawn to all of the abundant provisions the Father has provided for us in Christ.

In a life of worship, we will find ourselves in one of three spaces:

SPECTATOR

This space is all about observation. It's where we are present but aren't engaging with His presence. We are like a slowed down hologram that has densified; we are in the room physically, but not really present spiritually.

This spectator space is a purely intellectual approach to connecting with God. It's more about entertainment than engagement. We are looking to see what we can get out of it instead of what we can give. It's about consumption as opposed to contribution. Here, our insecurities prevent depth.

PARTICIPATOR

This space is all about collaboration. We are worshipping in "agreement" with what everyone else is doing. If those around us are raising hands, then we join in too. Participation is a response to others' actions, or lack thereof. We become a thermometer that responds to the temperature of the room. Here, our insecurities prevent us from letting go. We still long to be in control and highly value our dignity.

LOVER

This space is all about fascination. We engage in a heart-to-heart connection that is astounded by our union with Him. We worship not for what we can get out of it, but from the privilege of what we can give to Him. Out of our fascination, we long to explore who He is and all He has done. We become a thermostat that sets the spiritual temperature of the room. Some gather around messages and doctrines, but we gather around His presence, knowing that the presence of God is one of the greatest gifts we have. Our security in Him allows us to be undone in His presence.

He is a King who is worthy of our worship. Becoming a lover in His presence takes us from worship to worth-ship. We sail on the sea of His unending love. Our private loving of Him ignites breakthrough in corporate settings of worship. Personal intimacy becomes overflow when we gather together. It becomes less about the song being sung and more about being undone in the midst of the One who has ravished our hearts.

WORSHIP OPENS UP WINDOWS TO GOD'S PROMISES SET ASIDE FOR US.

Let go. Allow yourself to revel in all that He has done for you. Immerse yourself in childlike wonder and awe that is not tethered down by religious expectations or what is considered an appropriate response to His goodness. He is worth it all.

SPEAK UP: DECLARATION

I declare the safest place that can be known is hidden in Christ, and that is where I reside. I have been made for depth. Worthy is the Lamb that was slain. God, Your presence is life. My heart is Yours and I long to know Your heart more and more. I reject fear and control and choose to be undone in Your presence. Like David dancing before You, I choose to be lost in Your reality, not my dignity. The worth-ship has come in and I have set sail with Your wind blowing me into the depths of Your love. You are worthy of it all!

THINK DEEP: MEDITATION

Song of Solomon 4:9, Isaiah 62:5, Psalm 106:1

Day 6: False Covering

Jesus does some interesting things in the Gospels. One of these thought-provoking moments occurs when he curses the fig tree in Mark 11. What did this little fig tree do to deserve that decisive death?

In order to understand this exchange, we need to use the "principle of first mention" and find out when a fig tree is mentioned for the first time in the Bible.

Some would assume that there were just two trees mentioned in the Garden of Eden: the tree of life and the tree of the knowledge of good and evil. However, there is another tree that is also shown to be present in the story.

Genesis 3:7- *"Then the eyes of both of them were opened, and they knew they were naked; and they sewed fig leaves together and made themselves loin coverings."* (NASB)

LOVE—NOT FIG LEAVES— COVERS A MULTITUDE OF SINS.

It wasn't until Adam ate the fruit that both of their eyes were opened. Once everything changed for Adam and Eve, they then sewed fig leaves together to cover themselves. Voila—a fig tree in the Garden, revealing three trees.

Fast forward to the town of Bethany (which means "house of figs") and Jesus is not just talking at, but actually "answering" the tree. Yes, in the Greek, it clearly states that Jesus was responding to this fig tree. Who knows for sure what it was saying, but it was enough for Jesus to give that fig-less tree a beat down.

Adam and Eve were attempting to cover themselves with the works of their flesh, which are pretty worthless. Our flesh was crucified in Christ. Jesus was killing a false covering that is riddled with shame, guilt, and condemnation, all of which do not exist in Christ. That fig tree was cursed all the way down to its roots, never to live again. Jesus was showing the disciples that shame was dead. It would no longer be our portion.

If we are attempting to display our falsely wonderful works of the flesh, we need to stop. Embrace the wonderful finished work of Christ and know that it is no longer we who live, but Christ in us. Love—not fig leaves—covers a multitude of sins. If we are feeling shame, guilt, or condemnation, then our thinking is outside the mind of Christ. It is impossible for Jesus to think about such things. He killed them and our old sinful nature. Jesus didn't come to fix us, He came to kill us and then make us new.

In Christ we are good enough.

SPEAK UP: DECLARATION

Shame has died. My old, sinful nature was crucified and buried. My flesh has been crucified with Christ. I no longer live, but Christ in me. I take off any false covering on my life. I put on the finished work of Christ. I put on the helmet of salvation. I have the mind of Christ. I declare that my works of the flesh are worthless. My works of faith are fruitful and they are energized through God's love. The fruit that is growing will remain.

THINK DEEP: MEDITATION

Galatians 2:20, Galatians 5:24, Romans 8:1-17

DAY 7: RESTFUL REVELATION

The first revelation Adam had of God the Father was not a to-do list. It was not about having dominion, multiplying, or being fruitful. Adam's first interaction and understanding of God was centered on rest.

The days in Eden seem to have worked a bit differently than our current understanding of how days work. In the creation account in Genesis 1, it repeatedly says, "And there was evening and there was morning." The days in Eden began at night, not in the morning.

All revelation flows from rest. We live in a culture that rests from work. It's a week of overexerting and collapsing each night and constantly looking forward to the weekend so that we can *finally* rest. God set us up to work *from* rest. What if we began to look at our days differently and saw them beginning in the evening? So when asked "What does your day look like?" we can simply state, "Well, I am going to start my day with eight hours of sleep."

Orphans exert so much energy trying to get what they have freely been given in Christ. We often emphasize the prodigal son who was lost outside the father's house, yet the older brother was lost *inside* the father's house. I am not sure which is worse. Is it worse to be lost and know you are lost, or to be lost unknowingly in the very place of your inheritance?

ORPHANS EXERT SO MUCH ENERGY TRYING TO GET WHAT THEY HAVE FREELY BEEN GIVEN IN CHRIST.

Orphans love to work and serve, but not to receive because that takes them out of being in control. Rather than allowing someone else to freely give them something, or allowing themselves to depend on someone else, orphans need to provide everything themselves. Lovers outwork workers every time. Rest is a weapon against darkness because the enemy cannot rest since it is only found in the Father. The enemy lives in constant toil and works to pull us into the same space. Religion gives toil a gold star of performance and a pat on the back for busyness. Busy simply stands for "burdened under Satan's yoke."

We are to walk through valleys and lie down in green pastures. Orphans turn this around by lying down in valleys and then walking through green pastures, unable to enter His rest but boasting in their toil. Enter

His rest today by receiving all that He has for you. This rest will cause us to be incredibly productive, fruitful, and content as sons in the Father's lap. Rest is available every moment of every day.

Speak Up: Declaration

I declare all revelation flows from rest. I reject busyness and chaotic thinking. I embrace love, power, and a sound mind. Toil is an old garment that has been tossed in the trash. Fruitfulness and tremendous productivity will flow from my life as I rest in the Father. I get to work from rest, not for it. My day begins with hours of sleep, which prepare me to work refreshed, reenergized, and full of ideas. Rest is available to me whenever and wherever, for the Father is with me.

Think Deep: Meditation

Genesis 2:2, Psalm 23:2-4, Matthew 11:28-30, Mark 6:31

Day 8: Prophetic Tension

Have you ever received multiple prophetic words about what God is going to do or what is going to happen, with different sources all confirming the same thing?

This often causes us to feel elated and float on fluffy clouds of glistening glory. Then, suddenly, we aren't gliding through life with ease like the day before. It's as if reality doesn't seem to be coinciding with destiny.

When God speaks prophetically, He is relating to our present what He sees in the future. It's future history. It's an act of conception that gives birth to destiny-laden goodness. In order to unpack the goodness, we will need to make some adjustments to properly align ourselves with God's view of us in the present and in the future.

This is where we enter into a dialogue with the Holy Spirit regarding our own preparation. We need to synchronize our life with God's vision of us. Prophecy introduces us to our next upgrade. But when prophecy comes into our lives and we remain unchanged, there is no room for fulfillment.

THERE IS NO FUTURE WITHOUT PROCESS. NO DESTINY WITHOUT IDENTITY.

There is no future without process. No destiny without identity. We cannot learn patience through acceleration. It can only be learned through persistence. In the place of divine tension, where we have prophetic words but the present reality isn't syncing with them, we must persist. This is where we have a head like flint and a heart that's soft.

It's not about focusing on timing, but on His presence. As life progresses, so must our relationship with God. In His presence is fullness of joy. Our perseverance must be joyful (Colossians 1:11). Otherwise, we won't learn endurance.

We must ask how we need to adjust our thinking in order to properly pursue prophetic fulfillment. When we meander the trails focused on our oneness with Him, we become more confident to walk out in the prophetic promises spoken over our lives.

SPEAK UP: DECLARATION

The promises of God for my life are continually flowing in my direction. Thank you, God, for revealing them to me through people, scripture, and direct revelation. The present and the future are closing in on each other. Your presence—not timing—is my pursuit. Lord, soften my heart and take away any callouses. Joy is my portion as I persevere toward prophetic fulfillment. I fully embrace any adjustments in my thinking that are required for the next level of my destiny. I thank you, God, that you speak today and love to share Your beautiful promises of purpose.

THINK DEEP: MEDITATION

Romans 8:25, 2 Corinthians 1:20, Colossians 1:11, Philippians 3:14

DAY 9: A WHOLE LOT OF OLOGY

Our theology shapes our psychology, which governs our physiology, which then impacts cosmology.

That is quite a mouthful, so let's unpack this a skosh. For the sake of simplicity, let's say theology is how we see God. Do we see him as good, agitated, abundant, stingy, task-driven, or full of love? This is the epicenter from which all things flow into and out of our lives.

Our theology shapes our psychology, which is our thinking. This is the maze of mindsets and patterns of thinking that are eventually vocalized and realized.

Our mindsets are largely impacted by our perception of God. It is imperative that we see Him correctly. The eyes in our heads are simply data ports, but the eyes of our hearts are heavenly ports. These are the true eyes we see through. Hope gives us the ability to see into the heavenly realms, and it naturally flows when we see the goodness of God. Our thinking should then begin to agree and align with His goodness.

Every thought has an energy signature to it. The human brain is composed of about 100 billion nerve cells (neurons) interconnected by trillions of connections, called synapses. These are *electrical* pathways.

It is either in dissonance (outside the mind of Christ) or in harmony (inside the mind of Christ). When we align our thoughts with His own, they flow in harmony.

OUR THEOLOGY SHAPES OUR PSYCHOLOGY, WHICH GOVERNS OUR PHYSIOLOGY, WHICH THEN IMPACTS THE COSMOLOGY.

The truth then governs our physiology. As our minds are renewed through the power of the Holy Spirit and the words of God, our bodies follow suit. Romans 12:2 says, *"but be transformed by the renewing of your mind."* The word used there for transformation is actually "transfiguration." That means mind renewal brings a literal change to our physiology from which His Light flows out. Our flesh begins to mirror our spirit man.

A renewed mind, then, allows us to be the light of the world.

When we see God correctly, our psychology is in harmony, which fills our physiology with light (transfiguration). Then this impacts cosmology; we are talking about the cosmos, or all of creation.

All of creation is integrated and interwoven together. There is no separation nor distance between any part of the creation, including us. We are, however, the only part of creation that is new. We are a new creation. Thus, all of the old creation is groaning for us to be revealed, the sons of God (Romans 8:22).

As we see God correctly, our thinking flows in harmony, our body is filled with His Light, and the cosmos is affected as we're revealed by our good Father.

SPEAK UP: DECLARATION

I declare that the eyes of my heart are flooded with light so that I can understand the truth. I can see the goodness of God. In every circumstance and situation, the goodness of God is on display. Thank you, Holy Spirit, for giving me power to see my mind renewed. I am not alone in the process. Reveal any mindsets that are in dissonance and help me find harmony with the mind of Christ. I am a new creation whose transfiguration affects all of old creation. Thank you, Jesus, for making me new and calling me to be the light of the world.

THINK DEEP: MEDITATION

Matthew 17:1-9, Romans 8:19, Ephesians 1:18

Day 10: Gold Dust or Bust

It's understood that God made Adam from the "dust of the ground" in the Genesis account. Most people picture God tossing up some dry, dusty dirt into the air and voila, man enters stage left.

But what exactly was the ground made of? Was it like the soil we have today? If we go and start digging up dirt anywhere on our planet, we will discover a commonality in all the samples: decay. All dirt contains decay, which is a manifestation of death.

However, at this point in scripture, there was no death in Eden. There was no sin, so there was no death. So if the ground wasn't made of dirt, then what was it made of?

In Genesis 2, we see that a river flows from Eden to water the Garden and it becomes four rivers. Genesis 2:11 tells us about the land and how the first river flows through Havilah, the land of "pure gold."

I'd like to propose something. What if the "dust" from which God made us was not the dingy, dusty dirt we find in our backyard, but something different? I believe the dust of the ground is from the land of pure gold. Yes, gold dust was our original design. After all, we were made in His image. We were inherently made to be glorious.

Among the elements found in the human body, gold appears on the list [http://www.datagenetics.com/blog/april12011/]. I've personally seen gold dust manifest all over people in meetings. Perhaps in these moments, God is saying, "Remember your origin." These manifestations cause some to be very uncomfortable. Don't worry though, we've been given a Comforter who can help us when we are not comfortable.

God didn't create trash, and He certainly didn't die for it. We are the apex of His imaginative power. We are the best idea He ever had. It wouldn't be a stretch to think, then, that He would use materials of a higher standard to form His prized and one-of-a-kind creation.

GOD DIDN'T CREATE TRASH, AND HE CERTAINLY DIDN'T DIE FOR IT.

It's easy to find the gold in others when it would seem God used it to form us in the first place.

SPEAK UP: DECLARATION

I declare I am valuable. Value is determined by how much someone is willing to pay and Jesus paid His life for me. He is worthy, and He has made me worthy. God created a masterpiece and placed a part of Himself in me. I have been made with and for His Glory. Every person has been made in His image, so I can find gold in every person. Part of my job description is to be a miner who finds gold in the life of every person who crosses my path. I declare that I can see myself and others the way the Father sees us.

THINK DEEP: MEDITATION

Genesis 1:27, 2:11, John 1:4, Ephesians 2:10

DAY 11: SEEING FROM HONORING

Many want to see the supernatural become a natural part of their lives. They want to see miracles, angels, and more. After all, God is supernatural. That's his normal, so it should be our normal too.

A good starting point to see more miracles is honor. Life flows through honor. Want to see angels? Then honor them. Before anyone starts freaking out, I am not saying to worship them. But it's equally silly to ignore them. God commands His angelic hosts, so when we honor His hosts and acknowledge that they protect us, minister to us, and perform God's Word, heaven starts opening up for us to see in greater measures.

If we're meant to honor angels, then we are definitely meant to honor people. When you see someone moving in wonderful gifts of any kind, thank God for their life and how He made them. This is not just about the "power gifts," such as healing and prophecy. These can include things like a person's fantastic administrative abilities, or their level of hospitality. Anyone can be honored for they are made in the image of God.

> # WHEN WE HONOR THE PERSON, WE BEGIN TO SEE.

When we honor the person, we begin to see. Honor is like heavenly eye drops that bring clarity and unveil the Kingdom of Light, which is a world of sight.

This also affects the impact made in the harvest. If we cannot honor those who are different from us, who don't think like us, or believe like us, we will have little influence in their lives. If we don't honor others, then how can we expect them to honor us and what we carry?

Let's begin honoring those around our lives, including our family in heaven. Angels, the cloud of witnesses, the four living creatures, and more are all a part of our family in Christ. Honoring the unseen will cause the eyes of our hearts to absorb some light so that we can see even more of the supernatural (Ephesians 1:18).

SPEAK UP: DECLARATION

Thank you, Jesus, for Your heavenly hosts that minister to me, protect me, and perform Your words in and around my life. I honor the angels that are assigned to people, to nations, and more. I look at all the people around my life and I honor how you made them, God. Every person who thinks differently from me and believes differently from me, I choose to honor them. Father, You have given me the eyes of my heart to see. There is no separation between heaven and earth. Distance and separation are illusions. Jesus, Your sacrifice ripped open the heavens and I have been given direct access. I expect to see more and more every day.

Think Deep: Meditation

Psalm 91:11-12, Psalm 104:4, Ephesians 1:18

DAY 12: ACTS 2 AS NEW

Many of us have heard the story of Acts 2, but not many understand the full implications of what was released that day.

What we read is that the 120 are praying in the upper room and then the Holy Spirit says, "Hello, let's begin." Immediately after, thousands of people come into the Kingdom as Peter boldly proclaims the truth.

It is not by accident that the 3,000 who entered the Kingdom that day in Acts 2 point back to the 3,000 who perished the day the law was given (Exodus 32:28). Acts 2:41 was the ushering in of a whole new age called the New Covenant.

Now let's dive deeper into what transpired in that room. In verse 2, it all begins with a sound coming from heaven, followed by a rushing wind that fills the entire house. After the heavenly whirlwind flows, we see tongues of

> ## ONE FLAME IS MORE THAN ENOUGH WHEN WE HAVE THE VERY SPIRIT THAT RAISED JESUS FROM THE DEAD.

fire resting on each believer. Everyone is then filled with the Holy Spirit and begins talking in other languages.

Each person had just one flame above them. A double anointing isn't required in the New Covenant, unlike the way Elisha received a double portion from Elijah in the Old Covenant. One flame is more than enough when we have the very Spirit of God that raised Jesus from the dead.

Beyond the baptism of the Holy Spirit, what people usually miss about Acts 2 is the presence of angelic activity. Psalm 104:4 says, *"He makes his messengers winds, his ministers a flaming fire."* This is talking about angels. In that case, the wind that rushed into and filled the house in Acts 2 sounds like an angel party.

But remember, angels are both messengers of wind and ministers of *fire*. Not only did the angels come into the room, it's as if they sat on everyone's heads, ministering to each believer as a tongue of fire. Hebrews 1:14 says, *"Are not all angels ministering spirits sent to serve those who will inherit salvation?"* (NLT) It's interesting to note that the idea of angels resting on each believer's head resembles a helmet of salvation.

Acts 2 wasn't just about the baptism of the Holy Spirit and the beginning of the church. It was also the unleashing of the angelic realm to partner with those who have inherited salvation. Jesus said angels are harvesters (Matthew 13:39), as shown by the thousands of people who entered the Kingdom this day. We cannot effectively reach the harvest without angelic assistance.

The body of Christ is entering a season where the awareness of the angelic realm is going to increase. It is going to be fun and very productive.

SPEAK UP: DECLARATION

I am living in the greatest age of all, the New Covenant. The Kingdom of God is advancing on the earth like no other time in history. Thank you, Holy Spirit, for empowering me with the same power that raised Jesus from the dead. I cannot help but live in victory. I can live in the continual baptism of the Spirit every day. I choose to drink in all of His new wine. Thank you, Jesus, that Your heavenly hosts are with me as I fulfill Your call on my life. The harvest is ripe and Your angels can help me see many coming into Your Kingdom.

THINK DEEP: MEDITATION

Psalm 104:4, Matthew 13:39, Acts 2:1-4

Day 13: Patient Ascension

We ascend in our awareness as we wait on God and meditate on His goodness. Isaiah said in Isaiah 40, those who wait would soar like eagles.

To prevent us from ascending, the enemy works hard (toiling) to make believers feel overwhelmed and consumed with the cares and affairs of a world that they are not from. Distractions and the continual hum of white noise all work to undermine our ability to find space to wait and meditate.

The enemy is never intimidated by our busyness, but he is infuriated when we exercise patience in our waiting. The enemy cannot be patient because it's a fruit of the Holy Spirit.

As we *make* time to wait and meditate, we find that the higher we ascend in our awareness of God, the more paradoxical things become. There is less space, but more room. Most of the solid, physical world is empty space. Yet, there is nothing empty in Him; there are infinite realms of discovery. As we ascend in our awareness of Christ, we begin to see and interact with a higher reality. A journey into more of Jesus is a pathway into planes of existence that are never-ending.

It's not through our works that we ascend. It is through His finished work that we co-ascended. We now need to become aware of that ascension.

THE ENEMY IS NEVER INTIMIDATED BY OUR BUSYNESS, BUT HE IS INFURIATED WHEN WE EXERCISE PATIENCE IN OUR WAITING.

Proverbs 21:22 says, *"A warrior filled with wisdom ascends into the high places and releases regional breakthrough, bringing down strongholds of the mighty."* [Passion Translation]

Those who rule in the high places function in dominion in the low places. We are seated in the highest realm of the heavens at the right hand of the Father. We now need to become aware of that reality, the place of throne life. To set our mind above is to mentally relocate ourselves to our highest place of existence.

It's time to soar.

SPEAK UP: DECLARATION

Thank you, Jesus, that I have co-ascended with you. I am seated in the highest place possible. I reject the pull of busyness. I can be patient since I have been given this fruit of the Holy Spirit. My waiting infuriates the enemy and elevates my reality. I set my gaze on my beautiful Jesus to discover infinite planes of existence and realms of truth. The more I come to know, the less I will live low. I declare I am a warrior filled with wisdom and am ascending into the high places to release regional breakthrough, bringing down strongholds of the mighty.

THINK DEEP: MEDITATION

Isaiah 40:29-31, Proverbs 21:22, Ephesians 2:6

DAY 14: A + S = DROP DEAD

Many of us have heard the story of Ananias and Sapphira in Acts 5. They lie about giving all the proceeds to the apostles from a land sale and they both drop dead—the irony being that they died on the very thing they lied about, land. I would like to propose what may have been going on beyond the surface of this story.

Let's start by looking at their names. Ananias means "grace." The name Sapphira comes from "sapphire," the gemstone.

In Exodus 24, when Moses received the 10 commandments, the mountain was covered in these gemstones, as it says that under God's feet was a pavement of sapphire. That's quite the walkway. In essence, sapphire was the foundation on which the Mosaic Law was received. There are even some who say that the stone tablets themselves were hewn from the sapphire, which is very interesting to consider.

ANYTIME YOU MIX GRACE WITH LAW, IT WILL ALWAYS PRODUCE DEATH.

Fast forward to Acts 5 and you have Ananias (grace) married to Sapphira (law). Anytime you mix grace with law, it will always produce death. Grace plus law always equals law. Paul said himself that the Mosaic Law is the ministry of death (2 Corinthians 3:7).

Then in Acts 9, there is a different Ananias who goes and prays for Saul, who is blind. Grace (Ananias) comes to Saul and lays hands on him, and then scales fall off of Saul's eyes. Saul then becomes Paul.

Pure grace will always help us see clearly, so that we can help others gain clarity. His grace enables us to reign in all areas of life (Romans 5:17).

Speak Up: Declaration

I declare that I live in the age of grace. There is no veil over my heart. I receive the grace of Jesus today. Not an ounce of earning was part of my receiving. Your grace has come to me free of charge. I can reign in all areas of life now. Grace is flowing in my direction, and I yield myself to its powerful current that's taking me places beyond my wildest imaginations. My eyes can see clearly for the day of grace is here.

Think Deep: Meditation

Acts 5, Romans 5:17, 2 Corinthians 3:4-18

DAY 15: PAIN AND PURSUIT

Our society spends billions trying to escape from, numb out, or cope with pain. I am not referring to physical pain, but the emotional impact of life events that are hard to process. These are inevitable, but they don't have to be harmful.

James said to "consider it PURE JOY when we face trials." There is joy, and then there is pure joy. It's the latter that can only be experienced in the midst of pain.

There is a realm of holiness in joy. Jesus endured immense pain going to and on the cross. Yet, it was the JOY set before Him that caused Him to endure. We, of course, were the joy.

Pain is an opportunity to pursue the places within God's heart that cannot be accessed except through pain. It's this journey that ushers us into the fellowship of His sufferings which can overwhelm us in the ecstasy of

> **WHEN HIS HEART BECOMES THE OBJECT OF PURSUIT IN THE MIDST OF PAIN, DESTRUCTIVE DISAPPOINTMENT CANNOT TAKE ROOT.**

pure joy. It is a reality that transcends happiness. Joy is eternal; happiness is temporal. Happiness comes and goes, but you can abide permanently in joy.

When His heart becomes the object of pursuit in the midst of pain, destructive disappointment cannot take root. After all, what we pay attention to will determine our thought life. When we set our minds on Him, it transforms our speech and behavior and ultimately influences our surroundings. What we internalize will be vocalized and then realized.

This means we cannot afford the downward spiral of introspection. We must aim our attention toward His heart.

If we have pain today, His heart is open for discovery and it is there we will find the fruit of our trials and full satisfaction. Pure joy is a delicious reality.

SPEAK UP: DECLARATION

It's OK when I am not OK. In my trials I can access pure joy. Jesus' heart is available to enter into. Pathways of pain become highways of joy. It is here I can feast on the fruits of my trials. If I feel weak, I say, "I am strong!" Disappointment is not my portion in life. I have a best friend who experienced pain and knows the pure joy of trials. I have a Counselor available at all times. I have a Father who will never leave nor forsake me. I am surrounded on all sides by an eternal family. Fruitfulness is inevitable.

THINK DEEP: MEDITATION

Colossians 1:11, Hebrews 12:2, James 1:2

Day 16: Circular Travel

We need to order our lives according to God's vision for us. Wisdom flows when we learn how to think like He does and work the way He works. Prophetic words are a piece of this journey.

Prophecy is relational. When we are Presence-focused, we cooperate with who God is shaping us to become. Prophetic words relay the person He sees in us. From there, that outcome is being drawn to us as we pursue His heart. It's a collision of future history with present reality.

Sometimes life kicks us in the pants and we might meander off the trail of our destiny. It is here at times where we hear a faint voice as explained in Isaiah 30:21: *"Your ears shall hear a word behind you, saying, 'This is the way, walk in it.'"*

When it comes to guidance, the Kingdom is more concerned with you having a renewed mind, rather than a full file of prophetic words. An unrenewed mind can only process information. It is a low level of living that is driven simply by human logic and reasoning. A renewed mind can process revelation and use wisdom to apply it. The mind of Christ breaks open the ceiling of human logic and reasoning. It takes an uneducated fisherman like Peter and releases wisdom

THE MIND OF CHRIST BREAKS OPEN THE CEILING OF HUMAN LOGIC AND REASONING.

from above to confound those much *smarter* than he was, as he shared with the council in Acts 4.

When God speaks prophetically to our lives, He provides a time for change as part of the package. These times of change will last as long as it takes for us to make the necessary adjustments for the upgrade. When prophetic insight comes into our lives but we remain unchanged, there is no space for fulfillment.

If we fail to respond, our lives will go on, but they will become circular. In God's kindness, He will allow us to keep taking tests because He so desires the upgrades and promotions to be released in our lives when we pass them. If your life has felt like running eighth grade track, then perhaps a response is needed. God is never looking at what is wrong in our lives. He is looking at the areas that need to experience Jesus. He is concerned about promotion in our destiny and upgrades in our thinking.

What must adjust in our thinking today in order to pursue prophetic fulfillment?

What must change in our relationship with God in this new season of depth?

Who do we need to become today to fulfill our destiny tomorrow?

SPEAK UP: DECLARATION

I have been given a world-changing destiny. The mind of Christ is available to me in all of my decisions. I function in eternal intelligence. My life is wide open to necessary adjustments in my thinking. I choose to cooperate with who God is shaping me to become. Future history is being drawn to present reality. Father, Your promises over my life are being drawn to me like magnets. I cannot escape the goodness of Your thoughts toward me. Father, Your clarity perceives my destiny. Holy Spirit, flood the eyes of my heart with Light, so I can see the hope of the Father's calling on my life.

THINK DEEP: MEDITATION

Isaiah 30:21, 1 Timothy 1:18, James 1:2-4

Day 17: Lain

Love and pain are intrinsically connected. Human reason and logic are afraid of love because it costs everything. If we are going to fully love, it will require us to be fully present and to unplug from virtual reality.

Following God's love will lead us to places that are utterly terrifying to reason and logic. But God rewards risk. This means that playing it safe is what's actually risky. Traversing outside the lanes of predictability will require trust. Love trusts. Logic is suspicious.

His love annihilates self-sufficiency and demands dependency. When we operate by ourselves, away from love, we enter a personalized prison that constricts, restricts, oppresses, suppresses, and leads to depression. Dependency upon Him, on the other hand, brings fluency in the languages of love.

HUMAN REASON AND LOGIC ARE AFRAID OF LOVE BECAUSE IT COSTS EVERYTHING.

God's love is higher than justice, faith, and hope. In heaven, there will be no need for faith and hope. Yet, love will remain. It flows through the eternal timeline.

If we are going to understand our oneness with Him and the love that made us, then pain will be part of that pursuit. We cannot love and not experience pain. Likewise, we cannot experience pain and not love.

Religious activity will not last on this journey. One of the byproducts of religion is perfectionism. This isolated cave of an existence will never allow a person to not be OK. If we are going to walk through processes of pain, we must understand that at times, it will be messy.

Love thrives in messiness. Have you ever seen a plant that didn't grow in mud?

Receive His love today. Be drenched in it. Then give it away everywhere you go. We have an infinite supply of love that will never run out. We might tune out from this supply, but His love is always flowing, always growing.

Speak Up: Declaration

I declare that I am OK. It's OK to not be OK at times. Jesus can relate to experiencing pain. He was betrayed, misunderstood, hated, and more. The fellowship of His sufferings is a special place I can enter into. This doorway opens up much glory over my life. I reject the need to understand. I have been created to trust. Whatever messes may be in my life, they are incredible soil for superior growth. I receive Your love right now, Father. I drink in all of its goodness. I am loved. I am accepted. I am not going to play it safe, for that is too risky.

THINK DEEP: MEDITATION

1 Corinthians 13, Galatians 5:6, 1 John 4:18

DAY 18: LIVING IN THE LOGOS

In John 1, Jesus is referred to as the Word. The Greek word that's used here is "Logos," which means logic. "Graphe" is a Greek word that refers to the written Word of God (Scripture). As we begin the verse—"In the beginning was the Word (Logos)..."—we see that the Logos (Jesus) predates the Graphe (Scripture). In fact, all of the Graphe reveals and points to the Logos. Jesus is the full representation of the logic and opinion of the Father. Jesus is the Father's mind made up.

As it says in Hebrews 4:14-16, we can boldly go before the throne of the Father because of our High Priest— Jesus—who represents God's opinion (Logos). We know Jesus, and therefore, we know the Father's opinion.

Jesus, who is the Word, divides our spirit, soul, and body with His double-edged sword (Hebrews 4:12). He wants every facet of our existence penetrated by His life. He is piercing our states of being so that in Him, we can move and have our being (Acts 17:28). He wants to lay us bare and naked before God—before the Truth.

JESUS IS THE FULL REPRESENTATION OF THE LOGIC AND OPINION OF THE FATHER.

This is not to simply embarrass or expose us. We started out naked—as shown through Adam and Eve—so He is restoring us back to our origin. This is where we are comfortable in our own skin, knowing the Father's opinion towards us as found in Christ. In this safe place—the safest place there is—we have no need for a fig tree leaf covering. He is our covering.

Let's allow our High Priest to bring His single, decisive stroke, so that we are fully aware of the logic and opinion of God (Logos). Because we can trust His Word, we can function in total confidence. It is a powerful thing to be able to boldly approach God, knowing His opinion towards us is good.

Speak Up: Declaration

Father, Your thoughts toward me are good. Your mind has been completely made up in Jesus. I look to You, Jesus, and know the opinion of the Father toward me is always good. Jesus, I give you permission to bring Your double-edged sword to penetrate my entire being. The logic and opinion of God are piercing my spirit, soul, and body. I am totally comfortable being laid bare before you, Father. I can boldly approach your throne knowing that your opinion is good. I love to read the Graphe because it's an opportunity to learn about and encounter the Logos.

THINK DEEP: MEDITATION

John 1:1-5, Hebrews 4:12-16, Revelation 1:16

DAY 19: DIVING DEEP

Do you remember being a child and diving into the deep end of the pool for the first time? The rush of adrenaline, your heart racing as you delved into what seemed like an endless oceanic trench?

Many people's relationships are like the shallow end of the pool. They are controllable and often tread boringly on the surface. God, however, designed us for relational depth.

Whenever we relate in depth, tension always takes place. Just like muscle mass can't increase without tension, relationships cannot become deeper or stronger without it.

Often, this tension surrounds the choices we make to be vulnerable, let others in, and receive their love.

When Judas betrayed Jesus with a kiss, it perfectly demonstrated his pursuit of intimacy without covenant.

ISOLATION IS GOVERNED BY DECEPTION.

The kiss wasn't a reflection of the depth of his relationship with Jesus, but rather it was an act of selfishness. He was trying to benefit from Jesus without investing into the relationship. In a shallow relationship, one person doesn't give the other any authority to speak into their life.

This is like an orphan who has a hard time trusting anybody. As a result, they want to constantly be in control of their relationships. It is difficult for them to receive someone else's feedback and allow it to influence their behavior—even when the feedback is from a loving place—since that will take them out of being in control.

Isolation is governed by deception. People with trust issues will naturally turn to manipulation to keep others from getting too close. Heaven, however, is attracted to healthy, deep, and honest relationships. When we let our drawbridges down and allow others to walk past our fortified walls, we will experience breakthrough. The depth of breakthrough you experience is proportional to the depth of relationships in your life.

Here are just a few good indicators of relational depth:

- Loving one another (John 13:34-35)
- Building each other up (1 Thessalonians 4:18)
- Honoring and being devoted to one another (Romans 12:10)
- Forgiving one another (Ephesians 4:32)

- Submitting to one another (Ephesians 5:21)
- Serving one another (1 Peter 4:10)
- Confessing sins to one another (James 5:16)
- Spurring one another toward good deeds (Hebrews 10:24)

SPEAK UP: DECLARATION

I have been made for depth. I reject shallow and controllable relationships. I choose to let my drawbridge down, inviting others in past my walls. I am not afraid of tension in my relationships. It will only make them deeper. Heaven is flowing toward my relationships as I explore the deep end of the relational pool. I am not a lone ranger. Family reminds me of my identity. I am not afraid of intimacy. I am a forgiver, a lover, a builder, and a submitter. My relationships will be a sign and a wonder to the world that I know Jesus.

THINK DEEP: MEDITATION

John 13:34-35, Ephesians 4:32, 5:21, James 5:16

DAY 20: DON'T SETTLE

Have you heard much lately about Abraham's dad, Terah? Probably not, right? Terah was headed to the promised land but chose to settle in Haran, which means "mountainous" (Genesis 11:31). Very little is written about the life of someone who settles.

When we come against mountains, we will either settle in their valleys or command them to move. A rationale-driven life will always settle for less, since unbelief is easily accessible from a place of reason. Settling is a manifestation of control. It is a place of small-mindedness that requires little to no risk.

Abraham, who was previously called Abram, refused to settle and chose to travel into the unknown. In Genesis 12:1-4 and 7, we see that God SPEAKS in verse 1, telling Abram to leave everything he knows for a then-unknown destination. Abram departs as he's told, and then God APPEARS in verse 7. God appears after Abram takes steps of faith. As we traverse into unknown places with trust as our companion, we gain more revelation of Him.

Abraham didn't know where he was going. We are not called to speculate, we are called to believe. The outcome is God's part. Our part is to abide. God's unpredictability means we have no security in what He is doing, we can only be sure in who He is. When we feel confused, distraught,

WHEN WE COME AGAINST MOUNTAINS, WE WILL EITHER SETTLE IN THEIR VALLEYS OR COMMAND THEM TO MOVE.

or as though we've missed it, a good question to ask God is, "What part of your nature am I not seeing?"

Confidence is the consequence of abiding in Christ. Trust and anxiety are incompatible, only one can be chosen.

Don't settle for good when amazing is available.

Speak Up: Declaration

I declare that I am not a settler. I don't settle by mountains. In Christ, I move them. I live by faith, so I traverse into the unknown with trust as my companion. I am not a speculator; I am a believer. I will risk because I know it is rewarded. I can't help but be ever more confident as I am with Jesus. I declare that in every area of life I will not settle. Jesus paid too high a price for me to live at a low level governed by control. There is a bright future before me and it's in my line of sight.

THINK DEEP: MEDITATION

Genesis 11:31, 12:1-4, 7; 2 Corinthians 5:7

DAY 21: BENDING THE SENDING

Jesus authorized 12 guys before they were Christians. We don't stop to think about this reality often. They didn't go through a 12-week discipleship course. There was no membership class they attended.

Jesus simply chose them to be with Him. Together, their highest priority was relationship with each other, rather than a relationship with a structure. Even though the Twelve were not all "Christians" as defined by common standards, Jesus still sent them out as His representatives (Luke 10). How many leaders today would send out people who aren't devoted Christians into their city to represent them?

Then there's the guy who had a whole gaggle of demons in Mark 5. Jesus and the disciples come ashore and once Jesus delivers the man from all the critters, he wants to get on the boat with Jesus and the others.

JESUS AUTHORIZED 12 GUYS BEFORE THEY WERE CHRISTIANS.

This was the perfect opportunity for Jesus to do some Discipleship 101 on the high seas. Yet once again, Jesus gives the instruction to go into the towns and tell everyone what happened. Notice that Jesus, in the same pattern as he treated the disciples, has commissioned a guy who literally moments ago had hundreds and hundreds of demons. This man was hanging around graves, barely dressed and in chains.

When Jesus and the Twelve come back to the towns, it's full-blown Kingdom come. People are getting healed in the streets and incredible things are taking place. This is probably because of this one guy who was dramatically changed. What would've happened if Jesus took him on the boat instead of commissioning him?

Perhaps, in our discipleship zeal, we are abducting people out of their natural influence. We are training people beyond their level of obedience and ability, thus paralyzing their capacity to impact the harvest.

It may be time to bend our concept of sending.

SPEAK UP: DECLARATION

I declare that the harvest is ripe. The fields are white. People are ready to encounter God. It's my job to catch fish, not clean them. Holy Spirit, change the way I see the harvest and the sending of new Christians and pre-Christians. Being in relationship is my priority. Structure is meant to serve relationship, not the other way around. I embrace the messiness and unpredictability of the harvest. I have a Guide who can lead me into the Truth no matter where I am. I trust God with my life, so I can trust Him with others.

THINK DEEP: MEDITATION

Matthew 10:1, Mark 5:1-10, John 4

Concluding Thoughts

I trust this 21-day journey has helped to elevate your thinking and open up your awareness of the infinite possibilities resulting from your co-ascension in Christ. You have the honor and privilege of living out child-like faith, exploring the riches of His inheritance, encountering the depth of His goodness, and receiving the Father's immeasurable power flowing toward you.

I am humbled and honored that you would read this guidebook. I pray the words settle deep within your heart, reminding you of all that God has done and all that you are in Him. You are seated with Him now as a new creation bringing heaven.

Go and live the ascended life.

ABOUT THE AUTHOR:

Since childhood, I have always been a dreamer, looking to the horizon and knowing there is more. I wasn't content with boxes, when I knew that I could fly above them. At the age of 17 I fully committed my life to Jesus. Through my relationship with Him, my dreams have become even BIGGER. He said ALL things are possible to those who BELIEVE.

Playing it safe is risky, so I have lived my life as a risk-taker. Nearly everything I have done has involved stepping out in faith and expecting something good to come out of it. I am a spiritual entrepreneur and a literal one too.

At times I have doubted, second-guessed, and fallen flat on my face. Yet, I have learned God loves and rewards risk. There is something exhilarating and frightening about stepping into the unknown and being able to do nothing but trust. God has proven Himself time and time again as trustworthy and faithful.

Now, over two decades after committing myself to Jesus, I am still taking risks and believing for the impossible. I am passionate about helping others see the greatness that God has deposited in them and become more aware of their co-ascension with Christ. I love seeing people have God encounters that break off limitations, low-level thinking, and powerless living.

I wear a number of hats in my life: husband, father, pastor, teacher, business consultant, missionary, son, and friend. For the past 19 years, I have sown many seeds into secular universities through campus ministry. Currently, my family and I are bringing the Kingdom to UC San Diego in beautiful San Diego, California. I enjoy living life with my wife Cecilee and our two amazing children, Eowyn and Liam.

Brian's Resources

BOOKS

Jumpstart

*Little Beans and
a Big God*

PODCAST

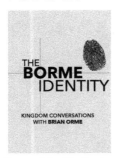

*Borme Identity Podcast
podcast.iborme.com*

*Find these and other great resources at:
iborme.com*

Stay Connected

📺 website   *iborme.com*

f facebook   *facebook.com/borme*

🐦 twitter   *@blondboybrian*

📷 instagram   *@borme*

▶️ youtube   *youtube.com/kingdomstrate*

in linkedin   *Brian Orme*

| For more information *iborme.com* | *join the mailing list* |

Request Brian to Speak

STUDENTS **+** CHURCHES **+** CONFERENCES

FOR
*Retreats, conferences, one-night gatherings,
churches, leadership events, and more*

CPSIA information can be obtained
at www.ICGtesting.com
Printed in the USA
LVHW050124070121
675887LV00019B/2889